# NIYAH L. BENSON

# SUHUDOO

Everyday wisdom for finding peace within

Copyright © 2019 by Niyah L. Benson All rights reserved.

This book or any portion there of may not be reproduced or used in any manner whatsoever without the express written permission of the author except for the use of brief quotations in a book review.

# PREFACE

*"I see life as a journey of possibilities and as I travel the road to the unknown, I realize that there is not one version of me but as many versions as there are possibilities in life. As life runs through its cycles just like the seasons and the music in my headphones there are however a number of recurring themes that can best be described by the melodies and lyrics that touch my soul..."*

SUHUDOO (NIYAH L BENSON)

## About the Author

My name is Suhudoo for a reason. Suhudoo is a Dagbani traditional name that means Peace. And when I look at it I find that it was what I always searched for and when I found it, it was me.

This book is for you and for all of us whom life has chosen to be seekers. A reminder that peace is the choice we make when we chose to be present to being.

# 1.

Every moment dies and gives birth to a new one.

And in every moment, you have a choice, to die and be reborn in harmony with life or to resist so that you can stay in a moment that no longer exists.

This is the trap of free will.

The idea that we can create or extend a moment that was destined to fall away.

The idea that there is a way to deserve such a moment by doing certain things.

Little do we know that it is not the moment falling away that becomes our pain but simply the idea that it should not.

This is how our demons are born, and this is how we run from moment to moment chasing the rising trying to avoid the fall.

For some people that becomes fear of commitment.

When we commit to something, we know that there will be risings and fallings with the things or people we commit to and we do not want that.

Niyah L. Benson

So, we run as soon as we fear the fall is on the horizon.

We run from one commitment to another, knowing that we want to stay but we can't.

We can't because we have forgotten how to fall with grace.

We have travelled so high that we fear that falling will take us into the bottomless pit from whence we will never emerge.

For some it becomes addiction to fantasy, either by feeding our system full of poisons that trigger euphoria or amnesia, or by hiding, burying ourselves in information so that when the fall comes, we are no longer presently aware.

For others who experienced the rise as temporary, it becomes a constant fight to stay at the bottom to avoid the disappointment of being on the rise only to end back down in the bottomless void again.

In every case the same thing is true - no matter how you run, you will always end up back where you started.

And always with a feeling that you missed something along the way, or that you must ever run faster to stay on top, or slower to stay down.

Eventually something will come along that kicks your feet from under you and forces you to stop.

It forces you to ride the wave as it is with no
means to run anymore.


And right there, when then running has stopped, and
there are no longer any choices to be made - right
there is the peace we searched for all along.


Harmoniously waving in and out of birth death and re-
birth, as we are born, die and reborn with it.

## 2.

The fastest way to judge a person's character is to not judge at all.

If you want to see who someone really is you must allow them to show themselves away from your expectations.

Likewise, those who really know themselves, do not worry about what they will do, instead they just are, as each moment require of them to be.

In the moment there are no mistakes, only the truth of what is exists.

# 3.

Part of finding your medicine is practicing becoming who you were always here to be.

As great as the mystery of finding the self is, it is only as far away as finding yourself in every moment.

# 4.

Often times the resistance in our lives is a result of a misalignment between who we perceive ourselves to be, our past and present environment and who we came here to express.

Knowing your ancestry, and reconnecting with your lineage allows you to connect your inherited talents and your ancestral story with your present situation.

From there you can work to heal those parts of your ancestry that affect you negatively today. You can then continue to build a future that is in alignment with your true purpose.

As you align, the resistance will fade and your life will begin to flow seamlessly

# 5.

The first thing that must happen is that we free ourselves from the hive mind mentality.

We learn to think, interact with and, evaluate reality for ourselves.

Learn how to extract valuable experience and information from the elevated elders and learned around us. Not, so that we can follow them blindly but so that we too can become learned elders one day - to be a beacon of light for those yet to come.

Who said what, is not as important as what was said.

# 6.

When you need something, the ancestors always deliver.

Just know that they see what is hidden from us and as such what they provide may not look in anyway how you envisioned it, yet it always turns out for the best.

They will take you on the journey you need to break you down and build you back up in a way that leaves you with no other choices than to move in the direction of your divine purpose.

All you have to do is be.

# 7.

Stop!

Slow down, be still, take your time...

Take a deep breath. Look around.

The point is not to get it all done, but to be fully present when doing it.

Come back to the present always.
Take care of what is here.

# 8.

Practicing what you preach is part of the package, when we are on a good run it is easy to give advice on patience and trust, but it is when we are going through it we really show who we are.

Always give thanks for the opportunity to rise and remember that the advice you give applies to you also

# 9.

Everything is a reflection of everything else, the state of the world can only be addressed by first addressing the state of the people living on it, and to address the people living on it you must first address yourself.

# 10.

The power of what was stolen from us, is greater than could ever have been imagined.

Looking back into the past to correct the future. - we must reach back through our ancestry to reclaim our birth right.

And as we do we rebuild our community, by becoming the best versions of ourselves.

# 11.

In order to excel we have to unlearn a lot of what was taught.

Something as simple as being told "if you take and test fail you are a failure", stops us from reaching any further.

The truth is that when you take a test and fail, you learn what you know and what you still need to work on.

And no matter how many times you have to go back and retake it, once you get 100% your understanding is as good as the person who took the test and passed with 100% first time around.

Life is not a competition of our ability to speed through tasks but rather a test of our determination to learn the lesson.

# 12.

** This one is meant to be read out loud. **

I love how I make me smile and how the jokes in my head have me cracking up for days.

I love how my smile makes me feel all warm and fuzzy inside.

I love how I pick myself back up after I cry.

I love how I can be so forgiving, and how much I really love myself living.

This day I give the greatest gift of all.

A declaration of pure unconditional love, to the one person who is always with me.

The one whom without my life would truly not be worth living.

This is my recognition of me, the greatest gift of love I will ever be.

# 13.

Spread love always....

Whether they deserve it or not, whether you deserve it or not.

Whether you feel it or not, especially when you don't feel it. Spread love always until love is all there is.

# 14.

Everything is growth... giving thanks for all the mistakes, the falling, the failing, the letting go aligning me with my truth and purpose.

## 15.

Social media is an excellent place for self-reflection.

What you read in the plain words of another, is a direct reflection of your own mental state.

We super impose our own mental state on the actions of others all the time, but it is not as easily recognized as when we sit behind a screen trying to communicate.

What emotion is produced comes entirely from your own imagination.

If we can take that learning and apply it to our day to day real world interactions, we have a pretty great indicator of what kind of mental state we are in.

And it becomes easy to see how changing our own minds can change both how we are perceived as well as how we perceive the reality, we are in.

## 16.

Some people will love your pain, some people will love your happiness, some people simply love and are happy that you are.

# 17.

As long as you keep fighting your current state peace is lost.

Instead observe the rhythm of life and learn
how to dance to its beat.

In the flow between discomfort and relief lies the
key to perfect peace and, if only you let her, life
will take you there effortlessly.

# 18.

Love between two people is simple, but we make it hard.

By withholding information, we deem irrelevant and or painful/unacceptable, we take away the right to choose on the part of the other person.

By practicing openness, non-judgment and acceptance of the real we can begin to form real relationships with those around us.

It is OK to be a private person, in fact being a private person has its value, but not with a person we would like to be intimate with.

Being private with yourself, withholding parts of your whole is the antithesis to intimacy.

Intimacy is the sharing of your whole being, openly and freely with another.

Not partial sharing of what you deem comfortable information, but the sharing of the fullness of your experience.

Niyah L. Benson

The intimacy and love that can then grow with a person that chose to accept you in your fullness is out of this world.

It is the divine love that we are all seeking.

Only by accepting ourselves for all that we are and allowing others to accept the same can we truly love.

Make effort every day to reveal yourself in your true light openly and without fear.

# 19.

Find what lifts your spirit and frees your souls,
do that as often as possible.

Let no thing, circumstance, man or no spirit block
you from what fills your being with joy.

You will be tested many times in many ways.

Stay focused, push through any blocks to get
back to your love of life.

The world needs your joy not your suffering.

## 20.

Be great, be confident, shine bright - not in competition
with others but in alignment with yourself.

Don't dim your light to comfort another, don't shine
your light simply to cast them into the shadows.

Shine because that is what you were born to
do, do so unapologetically.

Find your inner star and release it upon the world
in all its glory. Turn a deaf ear to those who try
to shame you into submission.

For they know not of the power their own light.
Shine bright, be great, be confident.

The world is waiting for you expectantly.

# 21.

Now that you've learned that nothing really matters, you must find your heart again.

You must open it up, against all odds, like a Lotus in bloom, you must fight the urge to stay submerged beneath the surface, hiding from life.

Life is an ebb and flow, cycling through stages of contraction and expansion.

Let go to learn all the ways in which you hold on, then hold on to learn about all the ways in which you were running away.

Do not go looking for comfort, or eternal bliss. Move instead to the pain and away from your desire

It may seem counter intuitive, but in so doing you may release the pattern created for you by circumstance and become the creator.
This is the true place of freedom.

The place where nothing matters yet everything is perfect.

Where nothing happens, but we find ourselves completely present.

Where all is love, yet each encounter is unique.

This place is not for everyone, but everyone is welcome here.

Once you arrive, you'll find this is where you were always. And whatever road you take from here, will return you to this place.

What you do once you arrive transcends all time and space.

It is the undoing of the doing, the return to being love in love as self.

# 22.

Introversion - blames self, looks for answers inside.

Extraversion - blames the world looks for answers outside.
Innocence - blames no one has no answers.

Ignorance - blames everyone has all the answers

Bliss - sees trouble and runs for the hills

Rage - sees trouble and runs into battle

Compassion - sees reality and offers a hand

Wisdom - observes the 'Self' doing all the above knowing that there is no 'Self' doing anything at all.

## 23.

Loving yourself has become somewhat interchangeable with stopping others from loving you or preventing yourself from loving others. Neither which are true.

To love yourself means to actively open up to allow others to love you, and actively opening up to loving others.

We are not isolated islands disconnected from those around us but rather a continuum of life expressed as being.

The love you give is the love you receive, and the love you receive is the love you give. One act of love feeds another infinitely ...

Love is not a quota or a scale you cannot give 1.5 love and receive 1 love back and as a result lack 0.5 love.

There is no necessity at any point to go looking for 0.5 love to fill the love deficit.

When you give love you instantly receive love because in actuality love is ever present and what may or may not be lacking is our ability to recognize it in the moment.

It's like the breath, even in the moments you are not actively thinking about breathing, as long as you are alive you are doing it. sometimes you may hold your breath because you actively distrust that life is supporting you or sometimes you may take extra deep breaths and feel exhilarated and the thought of being able to breathe.

Love is like that.

It is always where you are, constantly flowing through you and what varies is your awareness of it.

Self-love then is simply the recognition that you are love and loved every moment of your existence.

There is no condition that can make this not true.
Not now, not yesterday nor tomorrow.

Self-love is simply being and allowing love to express as you.

## 24.

Take note of all the ways in which you run away.

Sometimes we get so good at it we cannot see it in ourselves.

When discomfort arise take note, it is likely a reminder - whatever causes discomfort is something we have been running from.

When it is shown to you as an uncomfortable feeling, do not run away, do not try to find solace in things, people and thoughts.

Do not act on it. Just sit, observe and allow.

Watch the emotion roll in like a wave, pay attention to what parts of your body feel uncomfortable, listen to your thoughts without judgment.

When the wave finally subsides, interpret it like a dream.

What does it tell you?

What work is required on your part, what changes do

you need to make in the way you think, act and associate with whatever triggered your experience.

And if the answer is nothing, then do that.

We cannot change what is out of our control people, situations and past actions, but we can make peace with them.

We can decide to move in new ways, gain new experiences and let go of the people who no longer benefit our growth to create a new reality for ourselves going forward.

And if what you are running from is true grief/loss then allow yourself to grieve for a time, then let it go.

And if all else fails fake it until you make it.

Smile until smiling becomes a natural part of your being, give love until love is all you feel, beautify until beauty is all you see, let go and let go some more until all that is left is wide open space.

## 25.

What if instead of reloading the same movie over and over, we'd actually create a brand-new story-
...let's leave the old script behind.

We could call it Homo Transcendiu

## 26.

In a world where the defining and dividing question is, 'what are you?'

I wonder what would happen to prejudice if we chose not to define ourselves as a what and answer that question by the action we were performing in that moment.

Right now, I would be writing...

# 27.

Focus less on what you are going to do and more on what you are doing.

# 28.

Your life isn't about scoring as many points
as possible every day.

Although our whole western society is built around
competition, where everyone scrambles each day to get
one up on the scoreboard, this is not what life is.

Life is experience, pure and simple.

It is the observance and participation in life as
experienced through you.

Right and wrong are less important than finding
your own truth. Society status less important than honoring your ancestry.

The shape of the earth less important than
your experience while on it.

Living forever less important than living right now.

Being aesthetically beautiful less important than experiencing beauty in every moment.

Niyah L. Benson

The gift of life is not what you accumulate at the end, but the experiences you are having until you get there.

At the end, all is lost and life starts over empty of things, empty of knowing ready for a new experience cycle.

# 29.

Peace comes from recognition of what makes you peaceful, once found submerge into that.

## 30.

Gratitude and honor to all the obstacles in life, for they have been the greatest teachers of endurance, compassion and self-love.

# 31.

Maybe it didn't turn out as expected, or as you had hoped either way it turned out and that's all anyone can hope for or expect.

# 32.

Honor your needs, be it for inner peace or outer solitude.

De-clutter your sacred space, reevaluate your needs and reassess your wave form.

Take time to feel your feels, connect with your pains and find your truths.

You have grown, shrunk, stretched and contracted. Given, received, lost and gained.

Before the darkness turns to light once more you must trust that what has been has prepared you for what is to come.

# 33.

Recognize the need for peace and solitude, re-invent your inner circle ...

If you are here you are peace and if not peace you are inspiration.

In any case you are love

# 34.

Mind the words... they create your reality

# 35.

Deep breath in...

"It doesn't matter"....

Breathe out...

"It's all love"...

Repeat until no more energy is spent on things and people that drain you.

# 36.

Everything is perfect as it is and as it comes into being...

# 37.

Questions to ask when employing critical thinking:

Who said it? (Source)

Where/to whom did they say it? (Audience)

Why did they say it (Motivation),

What evidence is there to support what is being said? (Alternate sources)

How did they say it? (Medium i.e. Written, verbal, pictorial...),

When was it said? (Context)

Is it important?(Value)

When to use

Always when information is being processed
Why use it

Because stress kills and using critical thinking will reduce the amount of stress you experience by reducing the amount of time you spend emotionally invested in things that do not matter.

Love yourself, stop investing in things of no consequence.

# 38.

Don't give up your bad habits - add good ones.

There is only so much time in a week - eventually you will only have time for the good habits you're adding leaving the bad behind.

Try it with thoughts, actions and nutrition, add one new good habit every 3 weeks (it takes about 21-days to create a new habit) then do your math at the end of the year

## 39.

And so the house of cards is falling down and
a new chapter begins...

Focusing on the opportunities a new future will bring.

Out of the ashes like a phoenix bird I will build my
new house a top of a solid foundation.

Out of sorrow comes the recognition of joy in its true form.

All will be well in the end.

# 40.

Be careful of how you express.

Telling someone not to get big headed when they have achieved something great, or counteracting a good experience by adding something negative or negating a good experience all together is the beginning of the decent into negative thinking.

Allow yourself and others to be happy, proud or whatever positive experience they are having to the fullest.

There is no need for counter action in that moment and it definitely is not job to regulate what is.

If you feel the need to put yourself and others down in a moment of happiness examine your mind for the reasons.

# 41.

## Now is good

# 42.

In science when we measure something anything like, radio waves, light waves, length, weight etc we find the most sensitive device we can and use that for increased accuracy.

However, when measuring the human condition and human state of affairs we let the most desensitized humans tell us what goes and lock our sensitives into mental institutions. And then we ask ourselves why the world is a mess....

If you are of the type that insist that people should be less sensitive for your benefit and the benefit of the world, perhaps take a moment and learn something from the sensitives of this world because they are surely measuring something of value...

# 43.

Love is not something someone else creates in us or gives to us, it is not something we can administer, turn on and off or create and destroy.

It is not a person, a moment or an action. But rather every moment, action, thing and person exists in love.

Love is simply recognizing a thing for being a thing without passing judgment on how it does this.

It is just an observation of light waving in and out of existence and a recognition that you too are that light.

# 44.

The no stress mantra:

We cannot prevent the bus from being late but when it is we have a choice to either be stressed about it or enjoy the ride.

In the end It is what we do when we arrive that makes all the difference.

# 45.

Just as being married doesn't make you loyal and wearing a crown doesn't make you royal.

Being born in a place doesn't make you from it, and occupying land does not mean you own it.

## 46.

No words are truer than the ones that come
backed up by action.

All else are just space fillers and place holders.

We constantly seek to fill emptiness with somethingness,
to prove our good intentions, or to move something along in a desirable direction.

But the best intentions lies in learning to let the space
be and allowing things to evolve freely.

Once we truly learn this what becomes present is
without question what was to be.

# 47.

Mind your mind.

What comes to your idle mind will tell of who you are.

If deviant things occur in your mind explore where these ideas come from, how were they planted in your psyche?

Check what information sources, energies and people you keep around you to feed such thoughts.

Do a detox from external input for a while and observe as you change your mind.

# 48.

Q: When will I be healthy?
A: When you chose to take care of your body


Q: When will people and things stop bothering me?
A: When you chose to stop being bothered by people and things.


Q: When will I be free?
A: When you chose not to be controlled by your thoughts.


Q: When will I be happy?
A: When you chose to think happy thoughts.


Q: When will the world change?
A: When you chose to change yourself.

# 49.

Love, compassion and empathy... That is all.

# 51.

Trying to fit in to society while free spirited is like trying to fit the ocean into a glass of water.

A small part of you will fit. But the result is a fragmented and disconnected you.

Ever hoping that the glass will break, so that you can again be whole and roam free - only to be contained and touched by the parts of nature that naturally reach for your depths.

Some people fear the ocean, I fear the glass that tries to contain it.

## 52.

Healing is not comfortable.

It is rough, raw and bothersome...

It is a process of breaking down the old to build new.

It requires patience and understanding, that being whole isn't the goal - it's merely a byproduct of the journey.

The work of the healer is never done... and therein lies the beauty.

## 53.

I think humanities greatest flaw is our propensity to want to prevent all potential danger to ourselves and in our quest for the highest protection create the vast majority of dangers.

## 54.

There are no pure or impure thoughts ~ it's all just just thinking. S

ome thoughts linger and some are fleeting, some are conscious and some subconscious, some call for action others for constraint.

It's not what thoughts you are having but your level of identification with those thoughts that become the brightness of your light.

## 55.

Balance - the harmonic oscillation between active pursuit and passive acceptance.

# 56.

Pay attention to the subliminal messaging.

The ideas and core beliefs that lie so deeply rooted in the subconscious that you didn't even notice until someone else points them out to you or, you are forced into a situation when you do not have time to sensor your thoughts before expressing yourself.

Because you cannot see it doesn't mean it is not there. In fact, it is likely it exists in your mind exactly for that reason.

As such rather than being angry with a person who do note and alert you to them, be grateful, because without them how could you grow past the undesirable parts of yourself you didn't even know existed?

This is the whole issue with covert isms.

You are not actively whatever-ist. But you grew up in a system that taught you to be at your core.

The issue is not one of blame but one of being accountable for your own race biased demons and to face them head on when they come to light so that you can become the good person you think you are.

Everyone is tired all sides of the story. And we will continue to be unless we can get past our egos to work together to erase every trace of it in every mind

# 57.

The mind:

There's so much to do, so many places to go how will I find time for it all? I see these things that I want but I cannot have, I have these things that I'd like to be rid of.

The soul:

You are already that which has passed and that which will be. All converging in this moment, every moment. All that you need is in your reach and will be when you embody their essence in the now.

# 58.

Get out of your way and let happen... Step out of the doing and let be

# 59.

To find stillness of mind during times of change become the wave instead of the navigator.

# 60.

Stand in your own light without fear of blinding anyone.

Trust that yours will ignite the light of others.

# 61.

It's ok to fall a little, to fail a little. Do not hide from your demons - pull them into the light & watch them fade to dust.

# 62.

Time to hibernate...

## 63.

It's funny how no matter how much you try walking in straight lines life has a way of bringing us back full circle. It all makes sense when we look at the complete picture

# 64.

I had so much I wanted to say so I stayed silent and in the silence, I found relief from the need to speak at all...

# 65.

## Goddess Invocation

I am goddess in the flesh. I am electric, magnetic. I attract support, respect and reverence from those I meet. I speak my mind from the heart, with words of empowerment and love. I speak softly, for my power is not in the force of my voice but in the depth of my emotion.

I am goddess in the flesh. I am the moon shining light in the darkness. I reflect the light of my sun(s). I soften the hard of heart with my voice, nourish the hungry souls with my wisdom, heal the broken with my touch and empower the powerless through my vision.

I am goddess in the flesh. I am the mother of all. I am the warmth in the home. The moist darkness that encourages life to grow. The purpose that every man seeks. The reason that every man fight. My gift is my compassion, my life work is my community and my sisters are my allies.

I am goddess in the flesh, without me nothing can grow, without me the land is barren, without me man has no purpose. And because I know this I walk in power.

## 66.

Let go, and when you think you have let go of everything, let go again until there is no more holding on to let go of...

Fight the changes or give gratitude, either way change is inevitable.

With gratitude, our heart and soul is free to flow like the river into the ocean, never questioning her purpose even as she is devoured by the deep blue.

The river knows her purpose is to soften the rocks, to bring moisture to the earth and to bring nourishment to the beings of the land on her journey, but at the end she must return to the mother and finally descend to the place where nothing lives.

By accepting that nothing is permanent we open up space for happiness in the moment whatever it is.

# 67.

Take a deep breath, hold, breathe out. Take one step, stop, continue on. Let every moment be a practice in letting go.

# 68.

Actively surround yourself with information, people & impressions from a variety of sources, backgrounds and environments to stay balanced.

# 69.

Every roadblock, every bump in the road of life is an opportunity to heal and transform.

Every illness an invitation to step up our game and drop what no longer serves us.

When you see that this is true, every challenge can be greeted like an old friend bringing gifts of joy.

Excitement at the journey ahead, for at the end of it there is great reward.

Whether we survive or pass no longer becomes the question, but rather the transformation the experience brings along the way is the gift.

That is the wisdom of the healer.

## 70.

Emotional intelligence can only be achieved spending time in our own silent company and can only be tested in the company of others.

# 71.

Life changes, sometimes abruptly and jarringly so, it throws you into battle with yourself, always you.

We may want to blame external influences for our less fortunate events, but the truth is in your darkest hour it is yourself you face and meet with.

Your major life events are there to allow you sit down and assess your relationship with yourself.

All the lies you've told, the things you've hid from and the pain you've caused yourself.

It is your chance to make amends, to start a fresh new relationship with your own light and to learn to place yourself in the first room of love.

Once you do the healing may begin in truth.

# 71.

I am a reflection of you, look into my soul, what you see is the universe looking back at you in awe...

# 72.

It is so easy to be grateful when things go well.
We thank our lucky stars for all the laughs, prosperity and security. Life is good.

But today give thanks for the challenges and hard times.

They are the periods of time that grow your character, strengthen your reserve and prepare you for greatness.

Those are the times your true nature is revealed.

Give thanks for the uncertainty that gives rise to your creativity. For survival you will find a way.

Give thanks for the melancholy that inspires your art. Art that in turn inspires the world.

Give thanks for the poverty that teaches you how to be frugal. Cleanse your body from excess.

Give thanks for those who leave in time of need. Making room for those who won't.

Give thanks for the illness that knocks you down. Teaching you how to love yourself better.

Suhudoo

Today smile at your hardship and thank your ancestors and deities, gods and nature for trusting that you are ready to evolve.

## 73.

Free will can be a real blocker for some of us.

Having too many choices are almost as debilitating as having none, at all.

Sometimes our fear of making the wrong choice holds us prisoner.

We fool ourselves into believing it is our conscientiousness that prevent us from going in any direction, we believe that our ability to see how our choice may negatively affect some distant person in a distant future is what keeps us from moving, however in reality it is just another way that fear of commitment manifest.

In that moment of fear we chose nothing, and hope that we can stay floating between choices. But we know deep down that a choice will eventually be made for us.

Something we didn't want will manifest for us. And in that moment the blame game begins.

We blame life, people in it and a higher power if that is what we believe in, for making our lives less than desirable.

Suhudoo

Thoughts like "My life always..." starts to creep in and we huddle, disappointed and depressed over how "even though we are such nice people" life seems to always take a wrong turn.

When this happens to you over and over again it is time to take a step back. Take a deep look at yourself.

Are you truly moving towards your desires or are you simply staying still waiting for life to move for you?

Life will not magically manifest in your desired direction unless you let it know what you really want.

Your heart is your guide to your true desires and your mind is you tool for making them so.

When you find that thing, that you once in your innocence deeply desired but now when you think of it you dismiss as impossible, go there, do that.

Take a leap of faith and go into that fear and make that choice. Then trust that it will be so, even if you don't know how yet.

# 74.

Now let me explain something...
well actually I can't.

The only thing I can do is point at something and hope that you the viewer will be able to gather enough from my pointing that you eventually experience something.

But in actual fact in order for me to really point at something I would have to be pointing away from nothing.

Indeed, I would have to point in all directions at once including my own pointing device be it my finger, word or existence.

Now consider that for a moment. How do I point with a device at itself and at the same time point away from it in all directions without occupying all spaces and thus eliminating the very nothing i am trying to point away from? Well I cannot.

So how do I then explain? Like I said I can't.

Confused?

I hope so because in being so you might be closer to something than you have ever been before.

You see something is nothing in it's own right.

That's right.

Something is just a relationship, a distinction that we make in order to filter our experience into manageable chunks of nothing that we then use in order to experience something. See where that leaves you.... It left me with chunks of nothing.

Now let me explain nothing instead...

Well I can't do that either. Because I would have to point at nothing. But the mere action of pointing has left me in the land of something and not at all anywhere near the nothing i wanted to point out.

No matter how hard I try to point with my being be it with vocabulary, actions or anything else for that matter that I can think of all I will end up doing is leading you on a path so far away from nothing that you will end up back where you started. I.e. with big manageable chunks of nothing that you call something.

So where am I getting with this?

Hopefully nowhere and fast.

Niyah L. Benson

The point being that there is no point. No matter how you try to put something versus nothing in any argument. No matter how strong you think your argument might be for either something or nothing of that something you will end up with a mish mash of something and nothing which means anything.

Enter the great misunderstanding in all arguments.

The assumption that the other person is someone speaking on something rather than no one speaking on nothing and vice versa.

See we argue everything based on assumptions we make.

Mostly the assumption is that our experience is somewhat or entirely equal to the experience of the other. When that other uses pointing devices (words or actions) that you do not recognise you immediately assume this someone is wrong about something.

However, the fact is no one is right about anything.... The best we can do is to get as close to nothing as we can in our search for an experience of something, and in experiencing something we finally come to understand what 'nothing' is.

I know this will sound like gibberish to some and to some it will mean something. Again, case in point.

There is no one point and what decides is not my intention, your intention, the pointing device or any other such thing that we use to measure the reality of something.

One's experience determines what is.

And the experience is entirely based on the ability to cut up nothing into imaginary chunks that you call data or facts.

Then how well you compare your collected chunks of nothing with even more chunks of the same determines how well you seem to be able to reason, solve and act at any moment.

How close your chunks of nothing resembles the chunks of nothing someone else has collected will amount to how agreeable you find that someone. Someone who is actually just your perception of no one cutting nothing into imaginary chunks.

Absurd? Yes very.

But this is just one way of trying to explain to you how much of anything is actually down to your perception or experience as supposed to what some call a fact of a place called reality where something takes place.

Something versus nothing is what is absurd without a context to relate it to it just becomes a total mess as can be seen above.

You need nothing in order to point at something by the same token you need to know something in order to point at nothing.

Niyah L. Benson

Neither is better, higher, wiser than the other. But used within the correct context can actually have meaning within the context of experience.

This writing in and by itself is nothing created into something. Now what do you make of it?

# 75.

Love, light and balance has been a concept of mine that has over time grown into being a life philosophy.

Originally it was just love and light but as time grew on it was obvious that something was missing... balance.

So as so many have told me 'love, light and balance' is just another one of those things people say who want to sound spiritual but in reality, has no foundation in day to day living.

Well not so, at least not for me.

It amazes me how we as humans are so quick to draw conclusions about another and their ideas based on our own feelings about any particular subject.

When faced with a certain set of words or a combination of such we quickly decide whether we are going to listen or disregard everything said from that point on.

So, without further ado I will try to describe to you what love, light and balance is and how i came to adopt it not only as a fancy greeting but also as something I am striving towards in every and any situation life throws at me.

What is love?

This is a question that I have been asking myself ever since there was a self to ask the question.

It is something that have been felt since the beginning but over time has taken on various expressions positive as well as negative.

When I ask people define love, most will go on to talk about relationships in some shape or form. Some people will outright tell me they do not believe in love as if love was some sort of illusory idea that only exists for those who believe.

Others claim not to know what it means.

For me however love is...and it is as simple as that. When all other emotions are removed, we are a total peace and are not viewing the world through our angled self-fulfilling ideals what is there?

Well what I found was that there was not a void but a possibility.

It is a place of potential energy and when left alone this energy will ebb and flow undisrupted through our body system and give rise to a feeling of calm harmonious movement.

Suhudoo

This to me is love.

The basic energy that has the potential of becoming any movement be it emotional, physical or mental. It is attraction in its purest form, attraction being a force that moves us or steers us in a direction as supposed to another.

When all else is left out, all our preconceptions of what love does, should do, did not do for us, all thoughts on what love feels like and should and should not make us feel, and when any other subjective thought and movement is left out there is love.

Many people talk about pure love as being something that takes a particular expression but in my opinion love in its purest form just is. Nothing more nothing less.

Love just is?

Huh? So love just is? There is nothing I need to do or no one i need to project unto for love to be?

Exactly.

Love just is and therein lies its beauty. If love is the potential for all movement, emotions, motion, motivation and feelings then love must be in everything that we do.

Niyah L. Benson

In every thought that we have, every motion that we create, every emotion that we experience, every interaction that we have.

Then everything that is in motion must be in love...this then must mean that I am in love, am of love and do love all day every day without having to DO anything other than just be.

To me this realization confirmed what I have always felt in my very being.

No matter how much I was shaped into a person that said things like I hate this or that, or I dislike such and such in the end to me it was all aspects of one and the same.

What appeared to be an opposite emotion from love was in fact the same experienced from a different perspective. I realized that Hate could not be without love.

Hate more often than not if not always seems to be a direct expression of love. Love for something and not something else.

But what was even more important to me was that hate seemed to be something that existed only as a result of a desire.

As I searched through all the emotions, I realized that the same could be said for all them.

They were attached to desired events.

Even love as it was in my mind attached to the interaction between a potential partner and myself seemed to be just that. A desired outcome that either did or did not materialize.

But there was one major difference and that was when there was no desire for any outcome and all was left as is, love seemed to still be there. Only this time without any specific cause or direction. The direction it took was up to me.

Love is not a choice

So after all, when it dawned on me that love is not a choice and it is in fact in everything i do, be it good or bad, there was a choice to be made.

The choice was not to love or not, but what to do with this love that was there no matter what.

To me the choice was simple. And so then and there my journey recognizing that love is began with allowing love to be.

No need to search for any illusions, or pointers as to when and where love was going to happen because it was and is already with me.

What is light?

Niyah L. Benson

Well some say it is a particle and some say it is a wave form.

Some believe light is vision and clarity and some that light is just a separation from darkness.

To me light is what happens when we recognize a thing, place or experience. When we move from unawareness to awareness.

When a thing takes a shape and form and becomes something that we can process.

Light can be visual or spiritual, mental or emotional. In any case light is what we do when we move from one experience through the next.

Light is awareness in all it's shapes and forms.

I have had many discussions with people who believe that we came from a darkness and abyss of nothingness into something ness and that most is dark.

Well this is a way of seeing it. But that darkness or abyss of nothing ness is only so because we have yet to begin the experience of being aware.

And as such to me there is no such thing as darkness

only unawareness of the light that is there.

It is like when you open your eyes and begin to see, it is not that everything was dark around you it is just that you did not yet take in and recognize that light that was always around you.

And so light is not only vision it is also knowledge, understanding and wisdom.

Every shape or form that awareness may take may be equaled to light.

And so, my experience whatever it may be is that of light and my being is ever in search for new light and others see me through the light.

Balance

Our experience is one of movement through light. What is movement?

Well in essence it is a relative state.

For something to move it has to be something. For it to be something it has to be separate from something else.

How does it do that?

Niyah L. Benson

Well something is essentially a cumulation of mass into a compacted seemingly enclosed area.

This accumulation or compacted area whether it seems stationary or not is essentially made up of moving parts.

What makes it something is the relative distance of these parts in relation to the surrounding parts and their distances.

Once there is a something and a something else or something and its surrounding less dense parts, we can recognize movement.

As things move in relation to one another there is a pattern emerging.

A pattern that always strives towards equal distribution of parts so that no imaginary space or side is more filled with parts than another. But this is not a stationary balance.

It is a balance in motion. One-part moves making another move in another direction to accommodate the movement of the first. This is the balance.

It's an equilibria state. A waveform or particle movement striving to reach the ultimate distribution state but never quite reaching it. It is what life and all its components do.

And so, it is also something I felt necessary to adopt in my day to day living.

I recognize that there is a balance in everything. That ever event has its balancing partner not necessarily one that i may see or recognize at a glance but never the less it is so.

As such I decided to promote this balance by aiming for balance in my own actions and recognizing the balance that may come out of events out of my hands.

So, with love as my motivator, light as my experience and balance as my goal I travel my journey through life with a new set of tools. And thus far they have served me well in providing a better more productive experience than what was had before all this was realized.

So, I hope that this short writing has explained to those of you who question my motives and understanding of love, light and balance.

This is what it is, nothing more nothing less.
Take from it what you may.

# 76.

... I value you because you value love because love values all because all values one because one values completion because completion values inclusion because inclusion values me because...

# 77.

Now encompass everything that is at any given moment. Every moment is fleeting and in the now.

There is only now.

Whatever you do you do now.

Whatever you think you are thinking now. Whatever you feel you feel it now.

And since now is fleeting so are the things within the now.

Now is as long or short as your perception allows.

Some now extend over larger periods than others to our general perception.

But when you accept that at any given now the now that preceded and the now that followed are as different to one another as the now that is now.

You realize that it is all in your mind.

Even the now as you in reality is experience that now that already passed and are always processing the now that followed.

What this means is that there is only now and all things are here. Past, present and future happening at once.

# 78.

Between what is and what is not reigns the possibility of what could be.

Some minds search through what is not looking for possibilities, some search possibilities for the answer to what is.

Regardless of where you look the reality is, there is nowhere else you could be than right where you are

# 79.

Omnipresence is not being everywhere at same the time it is being HERE all the time. I AM

# 80.

When you see with your hearts that is me. I Am a reflection of the light that is you...

# 81.

LOVE between two souls feels not the presence of space-time...

## 82.

It is in the little things that we do.


Love doesn't have to be difficult or expressed in a particular way...it just IS - the foundation of every new day that dawns and every sun that sets.


It is the force that eggs us on to seek new horizons or to stay and explore the ones we already know.


It is there on the face of every being ebbing and flowing to the rhythm of our lives.


Often, we don't take notice of the love that simmers under the surface of every ordinary day.


But it is there transforming and creating within your life. And sometimes it stops it's activity and just IS...and it blows your mind way.

The split-second realization that love is inside of you and all around you.

Niyah L. Benson

It is in the last spec of light making it's way up the facade of that house across the road.

It is in the air that enters and exists your system as you inhale and exhale.

It is on the face of your children as they look upon you the center of their world.

It is in the chair that you sit on, the road that you walk and all your devices. It is in all that you feel and all that you experience.

It is you.

You are Love together with the rest of creation.

And when you stop and come to the realization that all is because of love then there is only one way forward and that is in love.

And that is where you find me. In love with the life that happens all around me all the time.

No matter the struggle I may face I face it in love and that struggle is my lover showing me how to be better, stronger wiser in my love.

Raising me one telling me to show what I got
and give more on top.

Challenging me to prove to myself that I am
love, in love and of love.

And in the end, all is well. For love is and I am, and we
are the union, the creation and life all in one.

And I smile in the presence of the love that IS ...

# 83.

Love is the driving force (motivator) at the base of everything that is (exists).

Love in its purest form is good in the sense that it maintains and promotes the life cycle.

But love as a manifestation through human experience takes on various expressions which we in turn add value to.

It is what is when we live life in the best way possible to promote and maintain life through our being.

It's all to do with the larger picture beyond me as a being.

## 84.

There are no permanent states of being...we are in constant flux.

Therefore, if you believe you are a thing you are not correct.

That thing that you believe that you are is either something you were or something that you will become in a moment in the future.

Attaching permanent labels to impermanent states causes confusion - on the one hand the label says we are something on the other we are actually in a moment doing something else.

For example, I may be a teacher between 9 and 5, but at 8 o'clock I am taking a course and am in actual fact a student, when my course finishes at 9 I go home to my children or spouse and I become mother/father and/or partner.

Likewise, we are not the things that we do, did or plan to do. When applied to trauma or unfavorable labels we've hoarded over a lifetime, this understanding can bring great release and healing.

It can allow us to break free from the belief that we are bound by past actions to forever be that which someone gave us in a word.

When the word was ugly, slow, lazy, stupid, mean, useless or something else hurtful, the understanding that those are all relative states to a situation and/or a person at the time and, are not representations of a permanent state that we are bound to, allows you to find new words to describe yourself.

If you find it hard to believe that being told 101 times that you are ugly does not make it a permanent fact, let's try this little mind experiment.

Take a moment and look at what you are doing right now. Describe it in a verb. Now that is what you are in this moment. Nothing more and nothing less.

Practice doing this as often as you can in a day.

Fill your mind with new vocabulary that describes you. At the end of the day think about all the things you were being in that day.

You will likely find that you spent majority of the day not being what you have been told that you are, or what you describe yourself as being, but in fact you were in constant movement between being this or being that.

When you look deeper you find that you were not being the things that you did, in fact you were being the very space in which the things were able to materialize.

You were being the potential to become ...
(Whatever you chose to be.)

And that is who you are.

The potential to be anything at all that your mind can imagine.

But first you have to undo the very thoughts that
make you believe that you are not.

## 85.

Most of our problems as humans comes from our ability to conceptualize 'what is not'.

We make laws/rules and regulations around 'what is not' to try and force what we think 'should be'.

'What is not' and 'should be' practically mean the same thing and as such we make it impossible to succeed at 'what is'.

## 86.

This morning a praying mantis reminded me
that it is time to come back.

Come back to your body, to love it again. To give it
attention, to nurture it, to beautify it because if you do
not it won't be long until it leaves this place.

So in spite of knowing it is not a priority, get my hair
done again, put on some jewelry and a little lip-gloss and
take some pictures in search of beautiful, not on the inside, but in the face that reflects to the world.

Reminded yourself that the feminine energy requires
access to the outer beauty to thrive.

It requires nurture in the form of what may seem
like 'superficial' things. It requires as much love as
the inside for a woman to thrive.

All this to say, embrace your my 'outer' beauty because there is
still work to be done and you need your body to be here for it.

And if you have lost touch with your outer

Niyah L. Benson

>                    beauty, please come back.

I see you, the world sees you but if you cannot see you and nurture you, your body will eventually up and leave.

Stay beautiful and nurtured on the inside as well as the outside.

The world needs you to shine with your brightest light.

# 87.

Always check yourself and your motives for doing anything.

If by doing what you are doing is not making you become, wiser, happier, healthier, more evolved, more passionate, more compassionate and more confident than you were before doing it then is it really in your best interest to do it?

If what you are doing is not building you up
then what is it doing?

Are you just doing it to prove that you can, if so why are you choosing to prove yourself through something that is not beneficial for you?

The likely answer is, somewhere in you there is a belief that you are not worthy of the things you most desire.

And by sticking around in unhealthy situations you are trying to find your worth so that you can eventually receive what you most want.

But here's the thing.

Niyah L. Benson

If you stick around situations that are no good for you, you are eventually going to become an expert at doing all those things that do not benefit you or your desires.

And even as you come to the realization that it is time to leave those things behind you will be left feeling inadequate in the direction of your greatness. You are digging a hole from which it is becomes increasingly hard to emerge.

So ask yourself if the situation is not making you wiser, happier, healthier, more evolved, more passionate, more compassionate and more confident in the direction of your dreams, then what are you actually doing it for, and more importantly for whom?

You are worthy of achieving your deepest desires, but only when you recognize that in order to achieve them you must pursue them and leave all else behind. Even the things that are almost but not quite it.

## 88.

The difference between a man and a woman is very subtle much more so than we make it out to be.

A woman and a man have the same purpose in life however how that purpose manifest through the energies is what differs.

Both women and men have the purpose of carrying on their bloodline.

Both women and men have the purpose of being providers and protectors of the future state of reality.

Both women and men have the same need to eat, sleep, procreate, commune, love and be loved.

A man's strength however is his force, his ability to stand strong against physical threats, to prepare a path and to remove any obstacles along the way by physical means, to foresee what may come in terms of physical/material adversaries and to eliminate them for the benefit of his tribe and his family.

A woman's strength is in her ability to seduce, to align the energies around her to face in the same direction.

She works on the subtle energies to create flow and power for the male energy to operate from, she foresees what may come in terms of emotional/spiritual adversary that may impact the male ability to exercise his strength for the benefit of her tribe and family.

Both men and women have access the to other within themselves. But only when the energy flows correctly between two beings of opposite poles do we become balanced beings.

You could say that the difference in a man and a woman is the directionality of these energies.

A man possesses female energy receptors inside of him it is what makes him able to exercise his force on the world by absorbing the energy she directs.

A woman likewise possess the masculine energy receptor inside of her, it is what makes her able to 'see' clearly what 'type' of energy and how much is needed in any moment.

When either of these are missing we become imbalanced.

As women we become chaotic, we will eventually try to create our own direction and feed our energy into ourselves in an effort to keep it moving.

Over time a woman starts to believe she does not need man to exist, she doesn't because she is a self-feeding system, she already has the energy and learns to use it to exert force on the world.

However her direction will be all over the place. She will struggle to achieve anything permanent because she is constantly changing where and how that energy is directed. And in order to achieve she will have to invert her flow inside out.

This is when she starts to look more and more like a man and over time, she will create the same energy needs as a man. She becomes a woman who only uses men momentarily to take care of those needs she cannot because of her lack of focus.

However deep inside all she really wants is a man to give her the queues she needs so that she can contribute to the shaping of a balanced reality.

As men we become lazy and eventually will try to conserve our energy by creating energy efficient ways of feeding the most basic energy needs.

Over time men will start to believe that all they need is to feed their basic instincts. He begins to seek out energy from several different sources, but in order to do so he too has to invert his energy and become seductive.

He creates a reality around him that looks strong and directional but in actuality he is just trying to get energy to be able to feed his most basic desires. Desires that have no purpose other than self-inflation.

He becomes a man who only services himself by acquiring as many women/followers as possible. Deep inside all he wants is one woman to give him the energy needed to build the strength necessary to mold reality in the shape of his purpose.

From this point of view we can begin to heal ourselves knowing that it is not what we do but how we energetically approach doing it that makes us imbalanced and incomplete or balanced and complete.

We need to come together as pairs not because we cannot survive and find a level of happiness momentarily without, but because we won't flourish and achieve a true sense of purpose until we do.

As for the idea of sister wives it is a matter of survival of the species. At times where, male populations are sparse we need a spread of the seed across many women to keep the DNA/ancestry diverse.

At those times females need to become communal around one man and feed his purpose so that he can be strong enough to protect and serve all of them.

At times where male/female population is balanced but infant/ child mortality is high we need to create more children in a one to one family structure. This is when we must protect our family unit above all else.

In cases where male population is high likewise it would be beneficial for women to have children by different men to keep diversity going. In this case women will have to be able to feed more than one man at a time and men become communal in their purpose/goal.

In our current reality it can be difficult to determine which is best. However, all of these constellations exist and can be beneficial only when we come at it from a basic understanding of our own true purpose and the medicine that we carry into the world.

Instead of trying to force other people to fall into your idea of which one it is, instead of focusing on what it should look like when they do focus on reconnecting with your ancestry.

Your ancestors and spirits are there to help you find where you fit in and in so doing find you the perfect partnership for the benefit of all.

# 89.

A most important thing to remember about the mind is that it processes explicit statements and positive statements before circling back to see if it is a to do or to disregard, a fact or something to aim for.

An example may be, "I will not be unhappy today" is processed as 'I am unhappy today' followed by "I aim to achieve this if anything else is true" followed by "disregard this".

The thing is the mind is unable to disregard the first two statements and so it will focus on "being unhappy today" and if that is not the case it will strive to achieve that state before trying to disregard the unhappiness.

When seen it this way it become painfully obvious that to our minds 'not' statements are oxymoronic. If it is on your mind it is there being processed and impossible to disregard.

This is why our internal language is reflected in our experiences. Someone who wakes up in the morning and says to self. "Today is a good day, I am happy today" has a greater chance of experiencing just that, than someone waking up thinking to self "Today is not going to be like yesterday, I will not be unhappy today".

In fact it is virtually impossible for the second person to experience anything other than what they said to self explicitly. I.e I am unhappy today and will strive to continue to make that true all day.

If you always keep this simple rule in mind, you are one step closer to creating the reality you desire simply by thinking it so.

Today is a good day, be happy today.

## 90.

Every challenge is an opportunity to heal or correct a behavior that no longer serves us.

When we see it in this way, challenges become blessings and those who challenge us angels (messengers) of the greater good.

# 91.

"When you stop being annoying then you'll stop being annoyed."

Nothing happens to you that is not of you.

It's sometimes a hard concept to swallow, because linguistically we call it being annoyed as if annoyed is external to us - however on further investigation you will find it is all you.

This is true for all emotions and when this is understood the possibility for being and feeling as a choice opens up the possibility of being at peace with all things.

## 92.

When it comes to lasting relationships love is only one part of the equation.

The biggest part is making the decision that this person is the one worth fighting for/working with and sticking the course.

When two people have the same commitment to the relationship only then does it have the potential to last a life-time.

# 93.

The worst disservice ever done to your being, was being told that there is something you have to do to be worthy of the best.

It is the opening into a state of being where instead of demanding high-quality things for ourselves, we spiral into a cycle of allowing more and more of the lesser things until lesser quality is all we experience.

No matter who, what or where you are, you are worthy of the highest quality spirits, relationships and experiences.

But until you realize and embody this you are in danger of falling victim to your own darkness. (Desires and whims, only there to masque the real issues.)

These are the things that you must demand (for yourself and embody for others):

*The best people

Those who support, uplift and protect you from harm

*The best nutrition

What nature provided or as close as you can afford

*The best health (Body, mind and soul)
Clean air, water, fire and earth.
Meditation
Relaxation
Introspection
Exercise
Travel
Education

*The best professional life

The things that fills your soul, energize you and support your comfortable living

* The best partner

Someone who love themselves highly and love you the same who would never allow 'unhealthy' people in their life or yours

*The best clients
The people who need your medicine/service and are able to accept and grow from it without leaving you with a cross to carry on their behalf.

Anything else is just distraction and potential dangers to your wellbeing.

If you focus on these, regardless of how you judge yourself currently eventually you will find yourself coming home to a place where you are at peace and joyful of what life has to offer, where you attract people who feel and act the same.

## 94.

If you do the work diligently there comes a time when all the things that felt like a struggle suddenly fall away to become just life.

If you are struggling to feel happy make it your everyday goal to inject happiness into every situation no matter how grim.

One day you will wake up and giggle for no special reason. You will meet adversity with a smile and deal with situations as they ebb and flow - finding yourself at peace with whatever is present.

The peace that exist in this space is that of the wise and traveled who knows the road can take any shape yet still never fails to see the beauty in the challenge of walking through it all.

Life is a journey of ups and downs, that when you learn to harmonize become a beautiful Melody of celebration

# 95.

Before trying to manifest your soul mate, you must find your own soul.

Align yourself with your star (purpose) and clean up your own ancestral karma.

Until then whomever you manifest will align with the very things you are trying to remove from your life, and cycles that you thought where complete will repeat...

## 96.

Don't fall asleep on your purpose.

This is the end of an era where our elders, leaders and inspired souls are leaving us with large gaps to fill.

Don't wait on the youth to grow into the gaps, we must keep it moving, carry on the legacy so that that those who have yet to come have something to carry into the future.

You must find yourself, your purpose quickly and move in the direction of your greatness.

Fill in the gaps where ever you fit in, inspirational speaker, healer, merchant, teacher, accountant philosopher, community worker, artist, politician, lover, supporter, mother, father, raiser of global consciousness, environmentalist, producer, scientist.

On your true path you are needed.

Let us not drop the ball, or feel discouraged by the swinging tides...

Instead focus harder on our individual contributions to the whole.

Ask yourself - Are you here to take up space wandering a lost soul seeking instant gratification, or are you here to fulfil on the purpose of your ancestry?

The answer is simple, yet the choice is yours.

The work you do is not for you, it is a contribution to the community and family all over the globe.

So, don't fall asleep on your purpose.

Find yourself quickly so that the work of those who came before does not become in vain...

# 97.

Allow yourself to be possessed by you, not other spirits, people and things.

When your ancestors walk firmly behind you you become your fullest expression, that is self-possession.

Walk your walk, talk your talk without trying to acquire or be acquired.

When you allow yourself to be possessed by you all things fall into place.

You become a being so complete and free that when people are in your presence, they too have no choice but to become free or seek elsewhere for someone to possess and be possessed by.

## 98.

Be a light unto the world, stay informed but not consumed by the atrocities you see.

If you are not in suffering you came to be the one to lift someone else out of darkness. Be that.

Don't dim your light in solidarity with another, there is no compassion in joining another in their pain.

Compassion is taking all your light letting it kiss the forehead of the ones still in the dark, giving them a beacon of hope that they too will rise.

So when you see suffering smile harder, love deeper and stay firm in your brightness.

This war is won when we all chose a higher vibration...

Flood the world with your hopes and dreams until your hopes and dreams become the world.

## 99.

You can struggle with your struggles, or you can simply be there as they happen.

The benefit of being present and aware rather than avoidant and distracted is coming away with the tools necessary to move on to greater things.

Always move toward your greatness.

That is where you will also find your peace

## 100.

Everything cycles, days, weeks, months, seasons, the moon around the earth, the earth around the sun, the sun around the galaxy, the galaxy around the universe...

Yet we are surprised when things return and even more surprised when they leave again.

Things that move will keep moving.

Peace is letting it be so.

## 101.

It is so much bigger than you...bare that in mind, always.

Let that guide every request you make to create a better reality for yourself and those you love.

It's never about you as a singular point but it is about the collective as a whole of which you are a part.

# 102.

When there is chaos or confusion the best action is
always to stand still long enough that you can see
clearly what you are dealing with.

When we react to the chaos we come from a place of the subconscious where all our fears and primitive responses reside.

The outcome in that case is never predictable
and likely to be less than desired.

When the subconscious action occurs, you are given an
opportunity to be courageous or be a coward.

The coward keeps running from it unwilling to examine itself.

The courageous on the other hand looks deep into the eyes
of the self, ready to take on the beast that resides within.

# 103.

Pay attention to your thoughts about life.

Many of your issues with life is not in how reality itself operates but in how you view yourself in relation to it.

Frequent thoughts of why me, that's not fair, I did this so life should respond like that are queues letting you know that you are in a mental state of entitlement.

Your state of entitlement has very little if at all to do with what is real. It is simply a way for you to bypass reality to appease an unrestful mind.

A state of entitlement is closely followed by feelings of resentment and anger toward an imagined culprit outside of yourself, the cause of your pain.

But the reality is you are the culprit and the creator of your own misery and the key is in the choices you make at every intersection.

No one owes you to be or act in any particular way just as you owe it to no one other than yourself to do the same.

No one has the power to make you do anything that you did not agree to doing, by way of free will.

Likewise, you do not have the power to make anyone do something they do not agree to doing, by their own free will.

When this is realized we can no longer be in a state of entitlement toward life and all anger and resentment falls away to be replaced by focused awareness and freedom.

## 104.

Remember who you came to be.

You did not come here to be a slave to higher spirits or people forever consumed by the bondage created by newly signed contracts.

Your soul for a spirit, your body for a house.

You did not come here to seek to acquire anything outside of yourself - stuck in an illusion of becoming elevated by something not already possessed.

You came here as a spirit in person with those who do not own a body standing behind you uncountable.

You came here as life expressing creation a perpetual force of manifestations creating new light.

Being is who you are, spirit is your source and purpose is your guiding star that moves you ever in the direction of your peace.

Suhudoo

Remember who you came to be are the people, places. spirits and things that set you free. Everything else are just illusions placed here to distract you.

# 105.

Loyalty is not about needing to create a reason to move on - always follow your star to where it needs to go but be honest with yourself about it.

You owe nothing but to yourself and your spirit to be in your purpose.

Loyalty therefore isn't about pleasing someone else by going against your being, but to be in your being while still supporting the path of another, especially when your paths are parting.

Being disloyal is really to put obstacles in the way of another to achieve your purpose or deliberately making a promise that you have no intention of keeping.

That is all.

# 106.

What is the difference between a rock falling on your foot and a person dropping the same rock on your foot?

You are the difference.

In the first scenario you'll likely take care of your hurting foot, maybe curse a little, but soon forget about it. Some may even tell an occasional anecdote about "the day a rock fell on my foot" usually followed by some light humor and laughter.

In the second scenario you curse a little then proceed to combat the person who dropped the rock before taking care of your foot.

You then go around telling everyone who has ears that a person dropped a rock on your foot, and 2 years later you are still telling the story.

Every time you see the person or someone who looks like them you go into a rage over the dropped rock on your foot, re-living the story over and over and over.

In worst case scenario you may even end up picking up a rock and throwing it on people s toes as a way to protect yourself from having another rock dropped on you.

Niyah L. Benson

Or get a gun a shoot the person in the face for dropping the rock.

Either way the story could move in a million different direction but the one thing that is true is that it will never end.

So you see, you create your own reality.

The only thing that is true in both scenarios is a rock and a foot hurting everything else is the story you create around it and how you chose to process it.

Suffering then is the creation of a never-ending story that ensures the painful past stay with you in every moment of your life from then on.

Freedom from suffering can only happen when you chose not to create a story and simply live in the moment.

Now for those of you who say what if the person who dropped the rock on my foot kills someone/me next time?

Well just like in the scenario where the rock simply dropped you were reminded to be present and aware in every moment.

Practice that without the need for a story.

# 107.

Feeling heard and seen, the most fundamental of human needs.

When you get to the root of most trauma, there sits a little person feeling invisible wanting nothing but to be understood.

This is why most healing happens not as a result of words being spoken, but by the presence we give at any moment in the silence between words.

## 108.

In this life you will have many teachers, and
you will teach many.

By devoting yourself to your path rather than the idea
of someone else's you will find that whatever you do
and where ever you go, whom so ever you follow and
those you lead will always be for you.

But if you forget to walk your own do not worry, there
will come a point where that walk will close and you
will have no choice but to return home.

## 109.

That time of night where everything is so peaceful, that you'd rather be exhausted in the morning than miss out on an opportunity to sit with yourself.

That time of night where the stillness becomes the backdrop against which your heart is finally able to speak its mind.

So I stay sitting in the dark, absorbing every word she speaks, so that when the morning comes we are able to start over in perfect alignment.

## Niyah L. Benson

*When the ancestors speak, listen... They do not care how you feel, but they do know what will get you to where you need to be. When the ancestors speak, there's not time to make sense, it is time to trust that they see something you do not. Just like parents know what is best for their children, so must we trust that they know what is right for us. This is the path of ancestral traditions. It is not about what you want...It is so much bigger than you.*

SUHUDOO AKA NIYAH L BENSON

Made in the USA
Columbia, SC
29 October 2021